Introduction

I took all the photographs in this book. They show a village in change over a per
came to Ecclesfield in 1950 it was already a suburb of Sheffield with housing estate
old Ecclesfield that still remained then has bit by bit been demolished or renovated. My photographs were taken with an eye to the future and hopefully that future has now arrived. If not and it lies further ahead then accept my apologies but it is now or never.

Photography is my hobby and local scenes are my subjects. I try to take clear sharp photographs but make no claim beyond that. Mostly I developed and printed my own work with lesser or greater success and the selection I have made for this book - hopefully - reflect the latter.

I am not a historian and the captions reflect my own personal memories or I have relied upon various reference books by people who are historians. However, photographs don't lie and they are the main purpose in compiling the book.

I pondered how to organise the pictures and decided to group them by streets where possible and where streets are long, as in the case of High Street, I have arranged them in the form of a walk proceeding from one end to the other.

I have tried not to be pedantic or critical of change. Not everything that was old was good. Nor can people be expected to live in poor conditions in order to maintain a rustic charm. Some of the old cottages and houses that have disappeared must have been dreadful. If plastering up the old stone walls made them more comfortable that must be accepted. But some demolition work was thoughtless and would probably not now be allowed.

Apart from that this is how Ecclesfield was during my residence. I hope it may be revealing to newcomers and reminiscent to older residents.

High St. Ecclesfield 1967

The northwest side of the square in 1963. Notable in the foreground are the cellars of the houses which formed The Isles - a short road running up the valley parallel to Townend Road. A magnifying glass on Kirby's small ironmonger's shop reveals that it was founded in 1924.

Bennett's was a grocer's shop. The block that contained it has now been altered out of all recognition.

This is a view taken from the grounds of Feoffees Hall in 1972.

This view of the square was taken from the back of Yew Lane in 1976. Notice that the red telephone box had been moved. Now it has gone altogether and a new BT box has been placed just about where the original one stood. I think that must be my Cortina in the centre of the picture.

Looking from the square in the other direction in 1962 Feoffees Hall stands high above. The right hand house of the pair was at one time the post office. Further to the right there is evidence of a cottage wall.

Feoffees Hall was built as a workhouse around 1730s. It served this purpose until 1852 when a replacement was built at Grenoside. From then onwards it became a new school to replace the one at the corner of Priory Road. In the photo on the previous page it is possible to see the housing for the school bell. The building remained in use as a school until it was replaced in 1894 with the board school which stood opposite the bottom of Sycamore Road. Feoffees Hall was demolished in 1968 to be replaced with a snooker club.

Where Yew Lane meets Stocks Hill there was a row of what I always understood were almshouses but I cannot confirm this. They may just have been old cottages. This is how they looked on 19 March 1968. Eva Ratcliffe House for pensioners now occupies the site.

Stocks Hill, going down towards the square and Church Street. The date is 1965. Court House Antiques Centre now occupies the building behind the signpost. The small shop on the right belonged to Mr. Wild, a butcher.

Looking now towards Priory Road and the old reading rooms. The date is 1962. The pub was The Tankard. It is only in recent times that its name has been changed to The Stocks.

This block is now Court House Antiques Centre. As can be seen it was a rather ordinary looking building back in 1971 when the photograph was taken. A visit to the centre enables visitors to see the superb roof beams which lay hidden for so long.

Here where Church Street meets Priory Road is a view of the old school (The shadow of the chimney marks the building). It was in use as a school until Feoffees Hall was chosen as being more suitable. Thereafter it became the village reading room until it was demolished in 1972. The two shops that, at the time, were in use as a chip shop and a greengrocery were at one time a public house named The George and Dragon. Both greengrocer and chippy have been replaced.

A closer view of the shops in the previous picture.
The photograph was taken around 1971 or 1972.

Demolition of the old school at the corner of Church Street and Priory Road. The year is 1972. The site is now part of Ecclesfield churchyard and has been grassed down. This is just one more example of local authority vandalism that was rampant in the 1970s. In this case the West Riding was to blame. I recall that one councillor was quoted as saying that he would not be satisfied until every ancient building in Ecclesfield had been replaced with a modern equivalent. An interesting detail in this picture is the swinging sign of the black bull outside the pub of the same name. This feature disappeared some years ago and is much missed.

Leaving Church Street to look at Priory Road, the photo, taken in 1968, shows cottages which have long since been demolished and where they stood is now part of the churchyard. The road was at one time known as Burying Lane for obvious reason.

This 1968 picture shows Hall Farm before the barns were demolished to make way for the houses and bungalows which were built later. The farmhouse is still standing but is now a private house. The name reflects its proximity to Ecclesfield Hall which is approached by the drive shown in the photograph.

Priory Road looking down to Church Street. Taken around 1972 the building on the left is nearing the end of its life and shortly after taking this photograph it was demolished. On the right is the entrance to an old alley. The shops on Church Street are still there but have undergone many changes since Mrs. Booker kept her village shop. The tall building was built as a house in the 18th century and was one of the largest in Ecclesfield. It is in elegant red brick and its three storeys dwarf its neighbours. It was converted into shops in the 19th century.

An old alley off Priory Road as it was around 1971. The building in the distance is said to be stables dating from the 18th century. The reason for the queue of cars is that a car body repairer used the buildings for his trade.

The footpath leads to the vicarage. This was taken in 1975 and is very much as it would have been at the time of the Gatty family. Beyond the path and to the left is the small graveyard for their family pets.

March 1979. Just when we all thought that winter was past a heavy snowfall took us all by surprise. It caused upset to many but was not entirely unwelcome as is shown in this snap.

Motorists found it hazardous, especially so at the awkward corner from St. Mary's Lane into Church Street - a terror to many a learner driver without the added difficulty of a snow surface.

Ecclesfield Church has always attracted photographers. A traditional view has been through the lych gate. This effort dates back to 1956.

Less conventional is the distant view on the right taken from Hunshelf on a misty autumn morning around 1975.

Remembrance Sunday. 13th November 1983

These photographs were taken around the war memorial.

18th August 1965. The photograph shows the demolition of the vicarage and its outbuildings, It was a shock to find that it was being demolished. The gentleman with the stick assured me that it was beyond preservation. That may have been so but in view of its literary association with the Gatty family it seems to have been a terrible mistake not to attempt to save it.

This shot of the drive also gives a glimpse of
the vicarage in its last days. Alfred Gatty,
Margaret Gatty, Juliana Ewing and all the rest
- R.I.P.

A yard in Church Street which must have been unchanged for centuries. Notice the pump for water and the hens running free. The exact yard is probably now unidentifiable. The date is around 1958.

The 1976 'Star' Walk passed Mrs. Coldwell's village shop. She was also licensed to sell "Ale, Beer, Porter and Tobacco". The shop closed and has now been converted to a dwelling house. It was more than just a shop but a meeting place with chairs for customers.

Ecclesfield Garage in 1973. It never looked to be too permanent and yet it survived many years, selling petrol and mending cars. A few years ago it finally closed providing a useful turning point for motorists who called at the chippy or post office and then wanted to turn round. To stop this little prank the earth movers came and built mounds of earth to keep them out.

This is St. Mary's Lane a little later in 1977 and looking in the opposite direction. The band hut can be seen at the top of the Lane.

GLOBE

In the 1970s two Ecclesfield businesses were neighbours on St. Mary's Lane. This picture shows Mr. Gillott's handyman's shop housed in a temporary building. In the days before B&Q these little shops could prosper. I remember that Mr. Gillott's father would cut board and wood to the required size using a hand saw. I believe that the family emigrated to Australia and the site became overgrown.

Just above the handyman's shop is the chippy. This is how it looked in the 1970s. I had a conversation with a man who had lived in Ecclesfield as a boy. Now in his eighties he told me that there had always been a fish and chip shop on the site, as far as he could remember.

Standing opposite the end of Yew Lane (known of old as Hill Top) was this nondescript brick faced building with tiled roof. When it was converted for use as a bakery an old cruck structure was revealed as shown in the photograph taken in 1984.

At the top of St. Mary's Lane at its junction with Yew Lane was the village chemist, old Mr. Nicholson. Before the advent of supermarkets and drug chains this was the place for prescriptions, patent medicines, not to mention films and film processing. After Mr. Nicholson's retirement and the building of the Mill Road medical centre a new and more convenient pharmacy was opened by Harry Allen at the corner of Mill Road and The Common in a one-time grocer's shop. This shop is now part of the Lloyd's group. Mr. Nicholson's shop became an antiques shop and latterly Pete's Pictures are in residence. The old cottage on the right of the picture was demolished in the 1960s.

This is the cottage mentioned on the previous page that stood at the top of St. Mary's Lane opposite Nicholson's chemist shop. Just beyond can be seen a small building which was at one time a second hand shop and at another a shop for the sale of motor cycles.

Where High Street meets St. Mary's Lane there stood two groups of cottages. The nearer pair are the older, dating from around 1800. The group of three beyond are Victorian. The whole group was demolished some twenty years ago and St. Mary's Close with its modern houses now stands on the site.

The photograph taken in 1958 shows a farm which stood at the corner of High Street and Yew Lane. It was demolished shortly after this was taken and replaced with the Eva Ratcliffe flats which now stand on the site. When I took the photograph I was standing in a clearing which appeared to have been the farmyard.

Crown House with its outbuildings is an example of an industrial complex going back to the 18th century. The picture shows it as it was in 1968.

This picture from 1972 shows the police station on the right next to the Rawson Infants' School which was later demolished. The police station was a poor thing compared with its modern counterpart on The Common but I don't know that it was any less effective - at least you could make contact by telephone. It was a saintly motorist who could claim that he had never had to cross this threshold with his driving licence and Certificate of Insurance.

Taken in 1968 the photograph shows a modest cottage and workshop. Situated on High Street and certainly 18th century it was built at right angles to the street which was common with older buildings. It has not been demolished but modernised and extended so that you have difficulty in recognising it if you did not know it of old.

Rawson Infants' School was the gift to the village of Hannah Rawson. In 1834 she gave the land and money to build a school for infant and junior children of poor parents. The building was enlarged in 1878 following its take-over by the Board of Education. When a new school for juniors was built at Wallet End towards the end of the 19th century the Rawson school catered for infants only. It was always spoken of as Rawson Infants until its demise. Then the Board school became the infants school and Town Modern became the junior school. When Rawson Infants was demolished a new building (No. 32 High Street) was built on the site. That new building is in use as an Occupational Health Unit at the time of writing.

This rather ramshackle cottage with its lean-to shops stood, in 1967, at the corner of Feoffees Road and High Street. Around 1980 it was purchased and renovated at which point a half-timbered Tudor cottage was revealed. The two shops were Ecclesfield's answer to a changing Britain. Mr. W. Slack added driving lessons to his role as shopkeeper. The other shop had the pretension of being a travel agent.

St. Michael's Field viewed from above Hartley Brook in 1979. This is the only open field remaining from the old village three-field system. It was still used as allotment plots when this photograph was taken. At the bottom of the picture is an early packhorse bridge which led up onto Cross Hill.

The photograph shows Ecclesfield Hall. There has been a 'hall' on this site since Tudor times but the present building dates from 1736.

On the left is Colour Sergeant Eric Jones of The Salvation Army. For the past twenty years, rain or shine, Eric has stood outside GT News on the High Street collecting for the Sally Army. He is well known to all the village, in uniform or out of it.

On the right the Rev. Ralph Mayland who was vicar at the time of the photo is having a rather heated debate with one of his flock. I remember it was a church open day around 1980 and something the vicar had done or proposed to do did not please someone.

The Priory is the oldest surviving building in Ecclesfield, parts of it dating back to the 13th century. Both the Priory and the Hall are visible from the back of the church but somewhat obscured by trees.

Ecclesfield Band on parade in May 1981. The band used to practice in the hut on St. Mary's Lane but now, alas, both the hut and the band are no more.

This view of 'The Minster of the Moors' was taken from a backyard in Yew Lane. The photograph dates from 1980.

Whether or not Whitley Lane can be counted as part of Ecclesfield I am not sure, but this is one of my favourite photographs. It shows an old red brick cottage standing at the entrance to the bridle way to Middleton Green. The cottage still stands but has been covered with cement. The bridle path has been tarmaced and made suitable for motor vehicles and the cow parsley has gone. The photo dates from 1975.

Ecclesfield cubs with their mums in 1980. They are gathered in front of the Co-op windows on High St. Later these windows were bricked up.

A view of the High Street, in 1967. The location is above and below Feoffees Road.
The gable that juts out was then the surgery of Dr Botros (see elsewhere). Below that a row of older terraced houses still stands.

This group of cottages was photographed in 1968. Centre left is the surgery of Dr. Labib Botros. Dr. Botros's surgery is not untypical of the type of surgeries used by family doctors before 1970. In fact he also had surgeries at 26 Crabtree Lane, 810 City Road and 282 Attercliffe Common (see 1959 Kelly's directory) It is interesting to compare them with the health centres in use today. The surgery was demolished shortly after this photo was taken.

Another view of this group of cottages photographed in 1968, the whole forming an unusual and very early group of buildings. The shop on the right, itself very old, is clearly a later addition.

The little shop that was attached to the older block: 'C & I Dunwell. Groceries, Provisions, Sweets, Tobacco' As interesting as the little shop are the outbuildings on the right of the picture including the ubiquitous workshop. The date is 1968.

The photograph shows what was at one time Singleton's Farm buildings. It is now the focal point for a thriving haulage business so that it is difficult to find a time when there are no lorries or wagons blocking the view. I managed to get this photograph on the 28th August 1985. These buildings are among the oldest non-religious buildings in Ecclesfield.

The Strange Mystery of The House and a Half. No. 95 - 97 High Street was of a most unusual design. It was sometimes known as Three Roofs on account of the gable and a half. The photograph was taken in the 1960s. Since then extensive work has been done to the property and it is now perfectly normal.

Mr Fellows' newsagent's shop is just another example of the fall of the small shopkeeper. In 1968 he had a flourishing shop. Since that time GT News has opened and also the Co-op and local supermarkets are selling newspapers and magazines. There are very few independent newsagents still in business. The shop and its neighbour on the left have both been converted to dwelling houses.

High Street opposite Sycamore Road. The Trustee Savings Bank is long closed and the shop which once belonged to Brightside and Carbrook Co-operative Society has gone through other uses. The school playground and shed in the photograph have been replaced with a new housing development. The date is 1980.

TRUSTEE SAVINGS BANK

Another glimpse of the blizzard of March 1979. This photograph shows its effect on High Street. It was taken near the junction with Sycamore Rd. A bus and a car seem to be in competition.

The Sportsman's Inn pub stood just about where the new library stands. When this photograph was taken around 1962 it was as shown. The old cottages on the right were nearing the end of their long lives. This is how the old High Street was before it was straightened. The area was known as Wallet End.

This location is the same as that on the previous page but the cottages have now been demolished leaving The Sportsman in isolation. The gap has revealed another old cottage. The Sixties marked the end of much of old Ecclesfield. That was when the village was run by Wortley Rural District Council.

Wallet End viewed in the opposite direction. The pair of cottages on the right were later converted into a single house which still stands. On the left the new straightened road obliterated the cottages to make room for the Ecclesfield Shopping Centre. The photograph dates from the early 1960s.

This shows more clearly what has happened to the old cottages in the previous picture. The road has been straightened, the cottages have gone and the new shopping centre has appeared. The date is around 1975. The camera is almost exactly on the site of the still-to-come library. The footpath leads to Sycamore Rd. On the right is the old Brightside and Carbrook Co-operative store. The Co-op butcher had the small shop next to the hoardings.

Primrose Cottage stood, in 1965, above what was to become the shopping centre. It too was demolished around the time that Primrose Drive was constructed and the farmland developed into a private housing estate. That would be around 1970.

The building of a housing estate on land which stretched from Wallet End down to Cross Hill greatly increased the population of Ecclesfield. This photograph shows the beginnings of Primrose Drive in 1970.

Here Wallet End meets Wordsworth Avenue. The pub sign belongs to the Greyhound. The cottage that opens on to the road was in a hazardous position at a time when this was quite a busy road for the new section of road had not been made.
At the corner of Wordsworth Avenue the waste land was later to be used for a complex of pensioners' flats. The date is 1968.

Wallet End just before widening. The two white buildings on the right were occupied by a cobbler and a bookmaker. Later they were converted to a chip shop. Just visible on the left behind the bushes was a greengrocer's shop, known to the locals as 'Dorothy's greengrocery' or more often just 'Dorothy's'. This part of High Street is now a lay by useful for parking. Date around 1968.

The old road and the new road can be seen here. On the extreme left is Wordsworth Avenue and on the right Primrose Drive. Ecclesfield Centre has been built but the supermarket section belonged to Mr. Braybrooke whose previous shop had been on The Common. The photograph dates from around 1974.

On the other side of Wordsworth Avenue stands Bank House, now much altered and housing the Regency restaurant. At the time the photograph was taken in 1968 it was owned by the Rushby family and old Mr. Rushby ran a nursery in the gardens behind the house. That was the place to head for your tomato plants, bedding plants or young dahlias. It was a pleasant trudge through the gardens to the nursery. Part of what was the garden is now a car park along Primrose Drive.

Townend Farm. In March 1980 Farmer Bingham decided to retire and those of us who lived nearby held our breath lest the land should be sold to a property developer. Fortunately a new tenant was found for the farm. There was an auction of items and the old haywain that had lain unused for many years finally disappeared.

Members of the Ecclesfield Brass Band would, on Christmas Day, tour the area playing carols and collecting for the band. This photograph shows them on The Wheel on Christmas Day 1975.

Whitley Hall Cricket Club's ground was and still is on Cinder Hill Lane. This is the old pavilion, now removed. The photograph was taken around 1979. I have a theory that the ground on which they play was at one time a dam. The Wheel is the name of a road close by - but where was the mill?

Broad Oaks cottage was once part of Broad Oaks farm. In the distance can be seen the back of the Arundel pub. Since the photograph was taken in May 1975 this has all disappeared to be replaced by another housing development. Certainly people need houses and there seems to be a shortage but it is sad none the less.

Viewed from Ecclesfield Park car park this foundry is now replaced by Morrison's filling station. The photograph was taken in 1977.

Ecclesfield Park recreation area in 1977. A see-saw is a traditional form of amusement for children though tame by to-day's computer games. In the background is Linden Terrace, popularly known as Nightgown Terrace. At one time five miners lived in the terrace along with their knocker-up 'Fanny Early Bird'. (Thanks to Mrs Dorothy Robinson for this information through The Church Magazine.)

In July 1978 we had a by-election. Ecclesfield, at that time, was in the Penistone ward. Allen McKay was the Labour candidate and to support him came Dennis Healey who was then, I believe, Chancellor of the Exchequer. He came to a meeting held in Ecclesfield Town Junior School. He is standing and the candidate is on the right. Allen McKay was duly elected in what was then a Labour stronghold.

This part of The Common is now Morrison's filling station. The photograph was taken during a particularly heavy downpour in July 1972 and shows that this part of Ecclesfield was prone to flooding. I believe this old factory building at one time was occupied by Green's Foundry.

Back in 1963 a friend who had newly acquired a single-lens reflex camera and who knew I was interested in photography came to me with the news that Oliver's Cottages were to be demolished. I did not even know of the existence of such a hamlet in the Ecclesfield area but I soon learned that it stood within the grounds of Brightside Foundry just off The Common on Green Lane. We went down, he with his new SLR and I with my folding rangefinder camera.

Another view of the Oliver's Cottages. The workshops were mainly used for the production of forks.

The interior of a workshop at Oliver's Cottages shortly before it was demolished. The anvil, hearth and bench are visible.

Beagle hunting dogs were used for hare hunting. In earlier days the pack were dispersed among homes in the village and brought together on hunt days. Latterly they were housed in kennels near the shooting range off Townend Road. Animal liberation activists released them some time ago. This photograph was taken on 9th May 1975 on the footpath between Whitley and Ecclesfield Church.

Near the shooting range off Townend Road.
This view looks towards the church,
beyond is industrial Ecclesfield